The
Management Guide
to
Negotiating

Kate Keenan

RAVETTE PUBLISHING

Published by Ravette Publishing Limited
P.O. Box 296
Horsham
West Sussex RH13 8FH
Telephone: (01403) 711443
Fax: (01403) 711554

Series Editor – Anne Tauté
Editor – Catriona Scott

Cover design – Jim Wire
Printing & Binding – Cox & Wyman Ltd.
Production – Oval Projects Ltd.

An Oval Project
produced for Ravette Publishing.

Cover – Like a delicate balancing act
successful negotiation strives to leave
everyone in equilibrium and harmony.

Acknowledgments:
John Barns
Gary Cheesman
Barry Tuckwood

Contents

This book is dedicated to
those who would like to manage better
but are too busy to begin.

Negotiating

Most people find themselves undertaking some form of negotiation every day of their lives, although often they do not recognize that this is what they are doing because they think negotiating is a skill which is only used by those making multi-million deals.

But negotiating is a stimulating way to arrive at an acceptable solution to the need for something, whether it is a need to resolve difficulties or to settle terms. It enables individuals to try to get what they want while giving others a chance to do the same.

This book helps you to understand how negotiating can obtain not only a better deal for yourself but also for those you deal with. It gives practical suggestions on how to go about making mutually beneficial agreements, thus enabling everybody to feel satisfied with the results and willing to negotiate another day.

1. The Need for Negotiating

Negotiating plays a vital part in whatever you manage. When what you want is under the control of others, it is not always easy to accomplish your ends. Nor, if you are in control, do others necessarily get what they want. In reality, neither side ever totally achieves what it sets out to achieve. But if both sides can arrive at an amicable agreement which more or less satisfies mutual interests, the negotiation can be said to be a success.

It is as important to know what you want to negotiate as it is to understand how to go about negotiating. Recognizing some of the hindrances which prevent successful negotiating from taking place is a good starting point.

Avoiding Negotiation

Negotiation is often seen as an activity which takes more time and energy than are available, so people may choose other less satisfactory ways of getting their way. For instance:

- **By command**. Telling people that a decision is not for discussion can seem an easier option than negotiating, though the long-term results are usually less effective.

- **By coercion**. Forcing people to do what you want may work initially. Not unnaturally, this builds up ill will and resentment, causing people to bear grudges and become considerably less co-operative.

- **By arbitration**. Allowing a neutral person to decide the outcome, rather than seeking a compromise, may seem an easier way out. But handing over the decision to an outsider often results in neither party obtaining what each really wants.

These methods of obtaining agreement and compliance are useful, but they rarely work as well as negotiation because people are not involved in agreeing the solution they have to implement.

Blockages to Negotiating

Many people avoid negotiation because they think it involves giving in and selling themselves short, or arguing, or being brow beaten into making concessions. All of these do happen but they are usually the consequence of not knowing how to negotiate.

Giving In

The reason you may end up giving in has to do with your own image of yourself. It may be because:

- You do not recognize that you are in a negotiating situation and assume it is the other person, not you, who holds all the cards.

- You think that by conceding you will please the other person involved.

- You do not think you have sufficient right to your requirements.

Giving in generally causes regrets later on, when you realize that a better deal could have been obtained. What is more, if you are negotiating with someone who needs to 'win', giving in too readily will be seen as a sign of weakness and affect your position in the long term. You should never give anything away without obtaining something in return.

Arguing

The main reasons why you might end up arguing are because:

- You allow yourself to be affected by someone's behaviour or remarks.

- You respond aggressively to what you deem to be unreasonable demands, or a lack of co-operation.

- You are expecting to engage in hostilities.

Argument usually means that both parties have confused the purpose of the negotiation with the personalities involved. If you refuse to respond to personal attacks and focus on the main issues, others will find it difficult to continue an argument on their own – although some have been known to try. It is important to remember that it takes two to have an argument.

Browbeating

The reason you may get browbeaten into submission has to do with how you perceive the negotiating relationship. For example:

- You feel you have to comply with the demands of someone who has a major influence on your business.

- You think that intimidation is par for the course.

Browbeating usually happens because you have allowed it to happen. It can help if you remember that people who make threats are often a great deal less sure of themselves than their behaviour would suggest. So sticking politely and firmly to your own case will prevent others from getting their own way at your expense. It is difficult to try to intimidate someone who shows no sign of being intimidated.

Seeing Negotiation as a Contest

Many people see negotiation as a contest. Logic dictates that if there are winners, there will also always be losers. But in negotiation, having 'winners' and therefore 'losers' is usually counter-productive. It prevents everyone from achieving the best possible deal because they end up opposed to each other.

People who consider conflict to be part and parcel of negotiation usually do so because they have not thought carefully about what it can achieve. There are several misconceptions which people may hold:

- It is all about getting your own way.

- It is all about obtaining the cheapest deal.

- It is all about beating the other side.

The problem with these beliefs is that they focus on getting the other party to agree to one specific target – often the lowest price. If this is agreed at the expense of other aspects, such as after-sales service, the negotiation will end up being unsatisfactory to both parties.

When the outcome is not mutually acceptable, the 'loser' will not be committed to the deal, so may not deliver what was promised on time or to the right standards. Ultimately a great deal of chasing and monitoring will be required on the part of the 'winner', who may now feel that not much was achieved after all.

Summary: Facing up to Negotiation

Fears about negotiation largely have to do with a lack of understanding about what it entails. Avoiding it means that you may never find out what an effective process it is.

The first step is to appreciate that negotiating is not a contest; it is an opportunity to establish good working relationships while obtaining a good deal. This can often form the basis of a strong bond between the two parties, which, in turn, can lead to long-term commitment.

When you seek someone else's agreement or co-operation to get what you want, negotiating is an excellent method to achieve it. Indeed, it is often the only means by which you can make the impossible possible.

Questions to Ask Yourself

Consider how you feel about negotiating, and ask yourself the following questions:

♦ Do I tend to avoid negotiating?

♦ If I do negotiate, do I usually concede more than I should?

♦ Do I get caught up in arguments?

♦ Do I find myself being forced to make concessions?

♦ Do I see negotiating as a contest in which there are winners and losers?

♦ Do I have misconceptions about what negotiating is all about?

If you answer 'Yes' to a number of these questions, you may need to examine your attitude to negotiation and/or help yourself to become more successful at negotiating.

You Will Be Doing Better If...

★ You are willing to negotiate.

★ You recognize that negotiating with people is better than commanding or coercing them.

★ You are aware that giving in usually leads to regret.

★ You appreciate that arguments need never happen.

★ You realize that intimidation has no place in negotiation.

★ You understand that winning at all costs is not the ultimate objective of negotiation.

★ You accept that negotiating is an excellent way to achieve agreement.

2. Understanding Negotiating

Negotiation is far more like a quest for the Holy Grail by all participants, than a gladiatorial fight to the death in the Colosseum.

It is vital to remember that a good deal is only a good deal when it is a good deal for both sides. So, successful negotiation is the process of getting what you want from others while enabling them to get what they want.

The Aims

The overall aim of negotiation is to obtain a mutually beneficial solution – a dovetailing of interests which gives both sides a degree of satisfaction with what they have agreed.

To achieve an acceptable solution there needs to be movement towards equity. This means people need to feel that there is a degree of even-handedness and fair play in the proceedings; and that the outcome of the negotiation has provided them with a reasonable reward in relation to what others have achieved.

The first important aim in negotiation is that it is felt to be fair. The second is to conclude an agreement which is seen as a square deal – of the sort a mother might make in order to guarantee equal portions of pudding to her two children when she says: "One divides and the other chooses."

The Situation

There are three negotiating situations in which you may find yourself:

1. **When it is in your interest**
   In this instance you are wanting something that another has the power to give; say, when asking for a pay rise.

2. **When it is in other people's interests**
   In this scenario others are wanting something that you have within your remit to give, such as a contract to provide you with office supplies.

3. **When it is in both your interests**
   Here, there is something you both want which is of mutual benefit and you have an equal stake in its accomplishment. For example, a joint project, where both parties will provide complementary skills.

In all three situations, understanding the relationship which can exist between the different parties plays an important part in being able to negotiate successfully.

The Power

Where the power lies is something that needs to be identified at the outset of any negotiation, so that you can work out how to react appropriately. Those who possess power can influence or force others to do things they may not want to do.

There are four principal sources of power which can influence the process of the negotiation. These are:

- **Your personality**. Being articulate, confident or charismatic are powerful personal qualities. If you possess such attributes, you are probably already quite good at getting others to comply. On the other hand, if you are dealing with a very persuasive person, you need to focus on the issues rather than the personality and not let this overwhelm you.

- **Your position**. Having position or status within the organization or business provides a source of power and authority. If you possess this sort of power, you can use it to good effect. On the other hand, if you are on the receiving end, it is important not to allow yourself to be intimidated by it.

- **Your expertise**. Having an area of expertise gives you the power to influence those who are less knowledgeable. Even a limited expertise means that people may assume you know more than you do. On the other hand, if you are confronted with the expertise of others, always ask for technical terms or jargon to be explained so that you are not baffled by them.

- **Your instinct**. Being able to recognize an opportunity when it occurs, or feeling that one is in the offing, can provide a powerful opportunity to exploit a situation and give you a head start.

It is worth taking time to establish the different sources of power individuals may have, because even if you believe a person to have the upper hand in terms of, for instance, status and position, you can often be surprised to find how much influence you may have in terms of expertise, or sheer personality.

In the three different situations in which you could be negotiating, who has the power depends on the situation. For example:

1. **Negotiating a salary rise**. On the surface, it would appear that all the power rests with the one who is able to agree the extra money. But it may be that you have power from knowledge gained by being with the company for many years and knowing things that others do not know. This could mean you are perceived as essential to the business and not easily replaceable.

2. **Dealing with a supplier of goods or services**. Here it may seem that you have the power because you are the purchaser. But it could be that the supplier has great personal power as a very skilled persuader and can sell ice-cubes to Eskimos.

3. **A joint project**. You may be the one who has created a big opportunity by developing a new idea while your potential partner has, say, all the right contacts, an excellent reputation, and financial stability. So a balance of power exists because both parties have something the other does not have and there is a vested interest in an alliance.

These different situations indicate that everyone has a source of power from which to negotiate. Power is never quite as one-sided as it may at first appear.

The Approach

In practical terms, wherever the power lies, it is how you approach negotiating that really matters. There are two basic, but opposing, approaches to negotiating:

- **The 'win-lose' approach**. This is the one in which each side is solely concerned to get the best deal for themselves, irrespective of the needs of the other.

- **The 'win-win' approach**. This is the one in which each side works to achieve an agreement which is satisfactory to both.

Both approaches enable deals to be made but leave each side with quite different feelings about the deal.

Win-Lose

This is the approach that many people suppose is what is meant by the word 'negotiation'. In fact, this approach relies upon the tactics of 'doing down', manipulation and pressurization. It assumes that whichever side holds out longest or is the strongest will be the outright winner.

The 'win-lose' approach is based on the premise that a defined, fixed amount is at the root of the deal – i.e. all that matters is how much either side is prepared to pay. Whatever is agreed, two things are certain:

- A relationship is neither sought nor expected to develop between those involved.

- One party or the other will feel aggrieved.

In the 'win-lose' approach, little trust is generated between the people concerned and each suspects the other of 'pulling a fast one'. Both parties feel a sense of inadequacy: the one who did 'worst' feels resentful and the one who did 'best' may consider that he or she could have got an even better deal with a little more effort.

What is more, if things go seriously adrift, a 'lose-lose' situation may occur, in which both parties come off badly or no deal is made at all. Thus a 'win-lose' approach always stands a chance of ultimately ending up as a 'no-win' result.

Win-Win

This approach to negotiating is the one generally used by those who need to work together. Both sides look for mutual gains to produce an amicable resolution. The main advantages of negotiating in this way are that:

- There are several solutions capable of creating a satisfactory agreement for both parties.

- Both parties have the opportunity to achieve what they want from the deal.

- The development of a longer-term relationship plays a strong, even desirable, part in the negotiation.

With the 'win-win' approach, contentment is part and parcel of the outcome. Each side relies on the other being committed to the deal that has been made – which tends to secure its success.

Summary: The Balancing Act

The aim of negotiation should be to provide both parties with a fair deal – like the equally weighted balance between the two arms of a scale. By regarding the process as a joint search for a solution, you will be more likely to achieve a successful result – one based on harmony and satisfaction.

Questions to Ask Yourself

Think about the different aspects of negotiating and ask yourself the following questions:

♦ Do I understand that the aims of negotiation are to provide an equitable and acceptable deal?

♦ Am I aware that there are three different negotiating scenarios?

♦ Do I realize that power plays a part in the proceedings?

♦ Do I understand that all parties possess some form of power to influence the negotiation?

♦ Am I aware of the differences between the 'win-lose' and the 'win-win' approach to negotiation?

♦ Do I realize that the 'win-lose' approach is rarely satisfactory?

♦ Do I appreciate that a 'win–win' approach enables everybody to get the best possible deal?

You Will Be Doing Better If...

★ You appreciate that the aims of negotiation should be to secure a fair and equitable outcome.

★ You recognize the various negotiating scenarios in which you may find yourself.

★ You can identify the sources of power with which you may be dealing.

★ You know where your own source of power lies.

★ You feel more confident about managing other people's power.

★ You understand the disadvantages of the 'win-lose' approach.

★ You appreciate why a 'win-win' approach usually achieves better results.

3.   Preparing

Negotiating needs to be thought of as two allies seeking an answer to a common conundrum. But no solution can be suggested unless both parties are clear about their objectives and the issues involved. So, you need to work out what you want, and think carefully about what others want, in order to be prepared for whatever may be proposed.

Working Out What You Want

To determine what, in ideal terms, you would like to accomplish from negotiation, you have to be sure of your goal. It might be an improved quality of life, or the desire to make more of your business. Once you have a goal in sight, you can work out the options which would enable you to achieve it.

If you do not have a clear idea of what you want, you are unlikely to achieve very much. On the other hand, even if you know precisely what you want, you have no guarantee that you will get it. The secret is to aim high but be realistic as to your chances of achieving your objective.

A good starting point is to evaluate your requirements and place them in order of priority in four categories:

- **The Maximum**: Everything you would like, if you could have it, including those elements which would enhance the deal for you, but which are really the icing on the cake.

- **The Minimum**: The objectives you must achieve if any agreement is to be arrived at.

- **The Trade Off**: The things you could afford to trade off or about which you would be prepared to make concessions in the course of the negotiation.

- **The Fall-back Position**: The alternative action you will take if a negotiated agreement does not prove possible.

By specifying what you want to accomplish in these terms, you obtain a sharper picture of exactly what it is you want from the negotiation and at what point you would actually walk away. For example:

The pay rise

You want more money so you have to have good reasons why you think you deserve it.

- **Maximum**. You are looking for a 10% increase in your wages plus a better office and state-of-the-art equipment.
- **Minimum**. You would not want to settle for anything less than 5%.

- **Trade off**. You might be prepared to trade new equipment for a few days' extra holiday.
- **Fall-back**. If you are not offered at least 5%, you will look for another job or make that career change you always dreamed of.

The increased need for a commodity

You want larger amounts of stationery so you have to identify a source of supply which can meet your requirements.

- **Maximum**. You want paper supplied little and often so as to maximize your cash flow.
- **Minimum**. You would accept buying some items in bulk, but would require a substantial discount.
- **Trade off**. You would be prepared to accept shorter credit terms, provided you could be guaranteed next-day delivery.
- **Fall-back**. If you do not obtain a satisfactory deal, you will shop around locally or consider going further afield.

The joint project

You and another company want to join forces to supply videos for the home business market. You have to make a detailed appraisal of your talents and the unique points your programme offers in meeting the needs of the person working from home.

- **Maximum**. You want the other company to take responsibility for the publicity, marketing and distribution while you create and produce.
- **Minimum** You require financial backing while you are developing the product.
- **Trade off**. You would be prepared to write the publicity copy for the promotion of the tapes.
- **Fall-back**. If the joint venture does not prove feasible, you could seek another partner, or carry on doing it all yourself by contracting your distribution to another company.

Working Out What They Want

To get the best from negotiation it is important to spend some time identifying the other party's needs. For this you have to obtain as much information as you can about their business to get as close as possible to understanding what their overall objectives are likely to be. This can be done by:

● Researching their background and present circumstances.

● Thinking yourself into their position and trying to deduce what it is they want to achieve.

● Identifying possible pressures with which they may be coping and how these could affect their position.

- Predicting the concessions they might make and considering what you might give in return.

- Calculating what might be of low cost for you to trade off but which would be of high value to them.

By posing a series of key questions, you can start to generate a list of possible needs. For example:

The pay rise
What financial constraints govern company policies? What else might the company offer in lieu? What is the going rate for this work at this time? Would paying you a rise be cheaper than finding a new person if you left?

The stationery needs
Is stationery at a premium due to world shortages and how does this affect paper prices? How regular is your order? How much local competition is there? Would prompt payment to the supplier improve their cash flow at little, if any, cost to yourself?

The joint project
How financially secure are your potential partners? Where might they have problems? What is their reason for wanting what you can provide? Are there any others they could approach if negotiations fail?

The more information you can generate about the other party's needs, the more likely you are to anticipate their requirements and understand the reasons why they may ask for certain things.

Making Contact

Your first contact enables you to find out more about the people with whom you intend to deal and allows them to find out more about you. If you are able to set up 'a talk about talks' and meet the other side informally, this will take away a considerable amount of the guesswork.

In addition to getting answers to many of your questions, it enables you to begin developing some sort of working relationship. The more people get to know each other, the more likely they are to begin to appreciate each other's point of view. For instance, if the negotiation is in your interest, talking with the other party, either face-to-face or over the telephone, gives you a better chance of feeling more comfortable when you actually come to negotiate.

It may not always be possible to meet in person, but you still have to exchange information which may be done in writing or over the telephone. If you cannot meet the people involved, it is essential that you take care to make a good first impression. Presenting well-laid out documents, which have been punctiliously written, will help to avoid the possibility of any confusion and indicate your standards of business practice.

When using the telephone, having notes about what you want to say to hand will enable you to keep to the point. This also indicates that you are clear about your purpose, and professional in your outlook.

Summary: Knowing What Is Wanted

Working out what you want in some detail enables you to assess how feasible your requirements are. Trying to second-guess the other side also has merits since it enables you to see things from their point of view. Making contact gives you a glimpse of how the land lies.

Preparing your case requires you to make a serious attempt to answer the following questions:

● What do I want?
● What do others want?
● What solutions might both of us accept?

In fact, arriving at the answers to these questions is what negotiating is all about.

Questions to Ask Yourself

Think about how you will go about preparing for the negotiation and answer the following questions:

◆ Am I certain of my ultimate goal?

◆ Have I worked out what my needs are and what I require in order to satisfy them?

◆ Am I clear about the minimum I need to achieve from the negotiation?

◆ Do I know what I am prepared to trade off?

◆ Have I decided on my fall-back position?

◆ Have I anticipated the other party's needs?

◆ Have I considered the sorts of concessions the other side might be prepared to make?

◆ Have I established contact with the other side before the negotiation begins?

◆ Am I aware that preparation will help me get what I want?

You Will Be Doing Better If...

★ You are certain of your needs and what you require to satisfy them.

★ You know the minimum you are prepared to accept from the negotiation.

★ You have identified the things you could afford to trade off if required.

★ You know what your fall-back position is.

★ You are prepared to work out what the other side is likely to be seeking.

★ You have some idea of the sort of things the other side might be prepared to trade off.

★ You make contact with the other side prior to starting the negotiation.

★ You realize how important preparation is.

4. Negotiating the Deal

Having prepared yourself and exchanged initial information, the next step is to negotiate the deal.

How you negotiate can make all the difference between a satisfactory and a disappointing outcome. First impressions produce lasting effects. So you need to ensure that the proceedings are opened in such a way that both sides are able to exchange information freely and express views candidly – which means describing the sort of results you are looking to achieve and your criteria for a successful outcome.

Proposing and Counter-Proposing

To open the negotiation, it is usual for the person who has already stated a position to make an offer which denotes the sort of terms that could form an acceptable settlement. For example, with stationery: "If you were to place a regular order, we could agree to 3% discount."

The important thing to remember is that nothing is ever given for nothing. This means that everything which is suggested should be dependent upon something being given in return, preferably something of equal validity or weight – i.e. "If you were to agree to this ... then I could agree to that."

Once the discussion is under way, there are a number of simple rules of thumb that will enable you to hold your own when negotiating. To do this you:

- Discuss the initial proposal first. Once an offer is on the table, no matter how useless you may think it is, you should discuss it in detail. If you make a counter-proposal immediately after the other side has put an offer on the table, they will still be waiting for their own proposal to be given a fair hearing, and will not be listening. Counter-proposals can only be effective if they refine or clarify the initial proposal.

- Explore the differences between what is on offer and what you want. 'You are offering a Tuesday delivery and we need delivery first thing on Monday." If you identify precisely where you differ, you can pinpoint areas where you might be able to make trade-offs to mutual advantage.

- Ask what the other party will be prepared to give in return – "Can you state what advantages that has for me?" To give away anything outright will allow others to grind away at your position by trying to obtain other concessions.

- Never take the first offer, even if it seems to be exactly what you want. If you agree too readily to something, you will always feel you might have done better. Taking time to consider what has been suggested prevents you from acting on impulse and possibly getting locked into a position from which it could be difficult to extricate yourself at a later stage. It is best to avoid agreeing to anything which you have not carefully thought through, however attractive it may seem.

Reacting to Proposals

There are some prudent ways of reacting to offers which get you further without committing yourself.

- **The negative response**. In this instance, you give your reasons before saying you disagree – "Because of x, y, z, I am unable to agree with that…"

- **The positive response**. Here, you agree with what with what is said, then give your reservations – "Yes, I agree, and I often feel the same, though it has been my experience….". To argue the case will only produce a bad atmosphere and inhibit progress. If you point out your doubts in this way, people are usually willing to listen. By altering the other party's perspective you can get them to see your position.

- **The conditional response**. In this instance, you agree but make it conditional – "I think that's a very positive proposition, subject to deliveries being made on Monday morning." If you qualify your reaction in this way, it has the advantage of requiring a reciprocal response, e.g. "Yes, that's fine" or "No, the earliest we could manage would be 5 o'clock on Monday."

Exploring the Options

To explore all the options related to offers, you need to find out more about the proposal and make sure that you have fully understood what is actually being offered. This involves asking questions for two different purposes: one to clarify and the other to verify.

Asking Questions

Before you agree to anything, you need to ask questions to clarify any points that are critical to the negotiation. "Could you explain what you mean by...?" "Can we go over the figures again?"

People who are skilled at negotiation tend to ask more questions than average. In fact, they will often start negotiating over the number of questions. "I seem to have answered several of your questions, perhaps you could now answer some of mine."

Asking questions gives you time to think and acts as

an excellent alternative to disagreement. It is better to get others to see any weakness in their position by asking questions about it, than by exposing the weaknesses you perceive.

If others seem reluctant to spend time elaborating, try explicitly signalling your questions. Say something like, "May I ask you a question about that?" By doing so you focus attention on obtaining the answer, making it difficult for the person questioned to evade the point since tacit agreement has been given that the question will be answered.

Verifying Answers

When people reply to complicated questions you may need to double-check the answer, because even when you think there is agreement, this can often prove not to be the case. "Can I just check that I've got this right? In answer to my question, you said…"

Another way to verify the answers is to summarize the exchange that has just taken place. "So, though we said Friday is the ideal delivery day for us, you are certain the earliest you could deliver would be Monday."

Checking what has been said helps to make sure that everybody's understanding of what has been discussed is the same as everyone else's. It is the only way to ensure that misunderstandings are avoided.

Noticing Shifts in Position

While gestures and facial expressions will indicate people's reactions (such as the involuntary grimace), it is their language (or lack of it) which provides clues to shifts in position. Listening to what people say, or do not say, can give you clues to the fact that they are changing their stance, and hint that some movement towards or away from agreement may be taking place. These are usually fairly subtle changes and can be easy to overlook when you are in the throes of discussion. For example:

- **A change of tack forwards**. Words such as 'never' or 'always' are modified to phrases like 'in most circumstances'. This suggests that there could be areas where things are less clear cut.

- **A change of tack backwards**. Points which were 'important' or 'needed attention' are now expressed in terms of being 'of major importance' or 'requiring careful consideration'. This indicates that entrenched positions could be forming in certain areas.

- **An omission**. Points which have been mentioned previously no longer form part of the discussion. This could signify a concession or the fact that this item is no longer of consequence.

Spotting these kinds of clues may give you advance notice of changing attitudes – possibly even before the other side realizes they have shifted their position.

Moving Things Forward

To enable ultimate agreement to take place, the discussion during negotiation should be advancing on all fronts. This means that the direction of any movement in your offer should be towards, rather than away from, the other side. Demands can therefore only really be reduced. If any attempt is made to increase demands because things are going well, this may prevent the negotiation from making any further progress. For example: if you say "So we've agreed on £3.00 a ream, haven't we?" and the response is "I'm sure we said £3.10", things are unlikely to move forward. On the other hand, if it is countered by "I'll let you have it for £2.95 if you'll agree to delivery by Tuesday morning", the deal has a much better chance of succeeding.

How much room for manoeuvre you have depends upon whether the outcome of the negotiation is in your interest or the other person's interest. For example:

The pay rise
As it is you who is asking for the pay rise, you need to have a number of alternative proposals to enable the negotiation to move forward. You will almost

certainly have to make more movement than the
other side.

The stationery deal

As it is in their interest to get the account, you can
afford to be less flexible if you do not get what you
want. It is the supplier who needs to move things
forward if you are to become, or remain, a customer.

The joint project

As it is in both your interests to form a symbiotic
association, each party needs to have a range of
options which can move things forward to a mutually advantageous conclusion.

Although the overall movement is forward in
impetus, at times each side will find it necessary to
re-establish its position and take time to explore
various side-alleys.

Seeing the Need to Compromise

Sometimes progress can come to a temporary halt
and requires a kick start. This is where making a
calculated compromise can play a productive part.
When doing so, you can offer those things you were
prepared to trade-off and even some desirable elements, while still protecting those that are essential.

Anything above a mid-way point between the maximum requirements and the fall-back position which you set yourself before negotiations began should leave you feeling that you have done well.

Being clear about the limits within which you are prepared to negotiate enables you to evaluate offers outside the range you were expecting. No matter how much preparation you have done, the other side may pull a surprise rabbit out of a hat. But it might be something so attractive that you would be prepared to modify one of your demands to conclude the deal.

Too much compromise all the way along could mean that you become dissatisfied with what you achieve; not enough compromise might jeopardize the negotiations to the point where you may not have a deal at all.

Closing the Deal

You have to make a positive effort to make a deal. It does not usually happen on its own. There are two ways you can do this:

● Summarize what has been discussed to show how far both sides have moved from their original positions in order to call for agreement on the terms offered.

- Suggest an adjournment in order to allow everybody to consider what is on offer.

With both methods you should take as much time as you need. You might, for instance, choose to summarize frequently, and you can suggest an adjournment as often and for as long as you require. By doing so, you are prevented from being rushed into agreement, or making a final concession in order to bring things to a conclusion which you may regret at your leisure.

Once the proposals have been agreed, one more thing remains: you need to make sure everybody agrees that you have all agreed the same thing.

Summary: Enlightened Negotiation

Negotiating can sometimes seem like attending a United Nations summit. Initially it may appear that there is no way anyone can emerge with what they really want. But by listening to and considering what others have to say, you are able to weigh up how things are progressing. By spotting shifts in positions, you can arrive at compromises and make it far more likely that the negotiation will reach a mutually beneficial conclusion.

Questions to Ask Yourself

Think about how you go about negotiating a deal and answer the following questions:

♦ Am I candid about my requirements from the outset?

♦ Do my proposals always depend on receiving something in return?

♦ Do I listen to and discuss the initial proposal before making any counter-proposal?

♦ Do I stop myself from taking the first offer, even if it seems irresistible?

♦ Do I ask questions in order to explore all options?

♦ Do I check that I have understood what is being offered?

♦ Am I aware when people are shifting their ground?

♦ Do I appreciate what compromise achieves?

♦ Do I make sure I have understood the deal before finally agreeing to it?

You Will Be Doing Better If...

★ You let people know what you are seeking.

★ You never make an offer which does not depend on something being given in return.

★ You only make a counter-proposal after listening carefully to what is proposed.

★ You never accept the first offer.

★ You ask questions and verify the answers when exploring all the options.

★ You notice when people are shifting their ground.

★ You are prepared to compromise from time to time in order to move forward.

★ You are certain that you have correctly understood the deal before agreeing to it.

★ You are content with the deal you have made.

5. Troubleshooting

However straightforward the negotiation process may seem, there are occasions when people become entrenched in their positions, try to take advantage by using underhand methods, or otherwise disrupt the proceedings. When encountering such obstacles you need to keep in mind and focus on:

- The matter in hand, and not the people.
- The intentions, not the behaviour.
- The needs of the parties, not their positions.

Concentrating on these issues will go a long way in helping you to keep things moving when the negotiation is not going as smoothly as you hoped.

Unlocking Deadlock

When absolute deadlock occurs it is usually because the negotiation has been allowed to drift away from the main issues, and has ended up concentrating on minor points on which people can all too easily take up uncompromising positions. You can unlock such a situation by:

- **Focussing on the purpose**. Returning to the original objectives of the negotiation can bring the proceedings back on course. "Perhaps we need to remind ourselves why we are here…?" This enables everyone to re-focus their sights on the purpose of the negotiation and will often remove the blockage.

- **Reviewing progress**. Showing how far the negotiation has progressed lets people see how much they stand to lose if the negotiation does not advance any further. "We have made good progress so far by agreeing…" In this way people are forced to appreciate what has already been achieved and encouraged to feel that it should be possible to sort the remaining difficulties.

- **Concentrating on the fundamental issues.** Concentrating on the fundamental issues can often get things back on track especially when it is the minor matters that have become the stumbling block. Very often it is trivial things that lead people to take up a fixed position. Yet positions which conflict at one level may be resolved if ways can be found for each party to achieve their objectives on another level. For example, in the negotiation over salary, getting more money (initial outcome) is only one way of obtaining a better quality of life (higher level outcome). There may be other ways of achieving a better quality of life if no extra money is available – such as longer holidays, more flexible working hours or better working conditions.

- **Asking 'What if...?' type questions**. Getting others to think of a way round the deadlock enables the discussion to be opened up again. For example, you could ask:

  - "What would stop this being a problem?"
  - "Under what circumstances would you be prepared to give way on this?"
  - "What if I/you agreed to ...?"

By asking people to speculate, the issues which are causing negotiations to founder can be looked at in another way. The answer can often put things into perspective and thus break through the impasse.

Employing any of these four methods makes it perfectly possible to resolve any deadlock by reasoned discussion.

Deflecting Dirty Tricks

Most people do not abandon their principles when conducting negotiations, but there are those who still think that negotiation is about using cunning and guile to take advantage of others. There are several well-worn dirty tricks you may encounter:

- **Not telling the truth** by withholding information, or only revealing a little in an attempt to trick you into believing that you are getting a good deal when you are not. If you check the facts before and during the negotiation, you will usually expose certain inconsistencies.

- **Using pressure tactics** by making additional requests or escalating demands when agreement is nearly achieved to try to make it more likely you will make a concession. If you keep repeating your own requirements in an even tone, people eventually give up as they realize they are getting nowhere.

- **Playing psychological games** such as enacting 'good guy/bad guy' roles (pleasant and nasty behaviour alternately), so as to make you feel stressed or apprehensive and therefore more likely to conclude the negotiation hastily. If you decline to respond to these ploys, they cannot have the desired effect.

- **Deferring to a higher authority** by inventing a phantom person to whom decisions have to be referred, such as a hard-hearted partner who is totally unreasonable and will be unlikely to agree to anything. This is a devious way of making someone else accountable for the deal, while appearing to remain moderate. If you call people's bluff and insist that the meeting is adjourned until everyone who is involved in the negotiations is present, you will find out whether or not this is the case.

Recognizing that such tactics are being used is the first step in deflecting them. The second is to expose them. For this you have two options. One is to state that you are aware of what is going on – "It seems to me that you're playing the 'good guy/bad guy' game." The other is to question the desirability of such behaviour in the negotiating process – "Perhaps these discussions might be better without conduct of this sort?"

The very act of letting people know you have seen what they are up to tends to stop them dead in their tracks, like confronting a masked highwayman with the words "Hello, George!"

Once you have challenged the tactics, you have to negotiate how you want the discussion to continue. "Can we now decide how to proceed on a more straightforward basis?" If the other side still will not behave acceptably, your best course of action is to defer the negotiation to another day, or quit altogether.

Curbing Aggression

Some people think that if they deliberately provoke dissension they will unsettle the proceedings and slant the outcome in their favour – for example, by attacking or blaming others; making sarcastic or derogatory remarks; pretending to take offence at what is said and then going on the defensive.

It is not possible to stop aggression, but you can curb it by keeping control of yourself. You do this by:

- Reducing your level of tension by taking deep breaths. Relaxing curtails the desire to retaliate.

- Looking calm and collected no matter what. Showing distress or disgust simply aggravates the aggressors and allows them to feel that their ploy is working.

- Not defending yourself or your position. Being drawn to give more, and necessarily weaker, reasons, simply provides ammunition for the other side.

If you do not allow yourself to get heated, you will avoid fuelling aggression and keep a door open to agreement.

Summary: Disarming Discord

The fact that others may act like bounty hunters intent on out-gunning the opposition does not mean that you should keep your finger on the trigger too.

You will get much further if you employ the tactics of the wise sheriff who takes the weapons away from gunslingers and expects them to settle their differences over a drink in the saloon, rather than reaching for their revolvers at the slightest provocation.

Questions to Ask Yourself

Think about what happens when trouble disrupts the negotiation and answer the following questions:

♦ Do I remind people what the negotiation is about by going over what has already been agreed?

♦ Do I prevail upon people to concentrate on the central issues rather than be sidetracked by trivial ones?

♦ Do I help people focus on their objectives when they are bogged down in entrenched positions?

♦ Do I ask people to speculate on how difficulties might be resolved?

♦ Do I recognize when dirty tricks are being used?

♦ Do I let people know that I know what they are up to?

♦ Do I keep control of my own actions?

You Will Be Doing Better If...

★ You know there are a number of practical ways to unlock deadlock.

★ You recap what has been agreed to remind people of the progress already made.

★ You get people to concentrate on the important issues and overlook the less important ones.

★ You focus on underlying objectives to help people get out of their entrenched position.

★ You expose those who are engaging in dirty tricks.

★ You remain calm, whatever happens.

★ You keep in mind that agreement is the ultimate objective.

6. Your Attitude to Negotiation

For negotiation to be successful, it is preferable to treat others as if they are acting in good faith and have entered the process in the right frame of mind to achieve results. Whether or not this is the case, you need to make sure that your attitude is positive and that your purpose is clear.

Keeping On Course

In order to achieve your aims you need to remember that you have every right to want what you want; and to keep in mind what it is that you want. This enables you to keep on course and allows you to decide whether what you hear suits you, or whether it is what you need. During the negotiation you should be:

- **Convinced of your own case**. This gives you confidence in your dealings.

- **Clear about your goal**. This stops you from getting distracted by smaller issues which might prevent an ultimate agreement.

- **Able to 'walk away'**. This prevents you from feeling you have to make a deal at all costs. To be able to make decisions without pressure, you need to believe that there is no deal you cannot do without.

If you can keep these things in mind, you will greatly enhance the chances of achieving your ends.

Maintaining Your Poise

You gain a moral and emotional advantage if you make sure that your behaviour reflects a constructive attitude, irrespective of how others behave. This can be demonstrated by:

- **Keeping your language neutral**. If you moderate your language by saying, for example, "The arguments you are putting forward don't seem to justify your needs" rather than "That's nonsense", you can forestall unwarranted conflict.

- **Being prepared to adapt**. If you are prepared to adapt when a proposal offers you much the same as you need – albeit in a different form – you may profit in ways you did not foresee.

- **Showing appreciation**. If you show your appreciation for the fact that people have compromised, made concessions or shown willing, it creates reciprocal good feeling and encourages others to continue to behave well.

Your behaviour plays a large part in preventing the negotiation from taking a negative turn. If you behave openly and reasonably, it is much more likely that the other side will follow suit.

Summary: Having the Right Attitude

Many people enter a negotiation with the attitude that everyone else is probably going to behave badly, so one more will not make any difference. But having the right attitude is vital if you are going to end up with a good deal.

By believing that others have entered the negotiating process in good faith, and by behaving with integrity, you set the standards for the negotiation that you wish to see maintained.

Your attitude will be exerting a positive influence on the proceedings and this may very well carry the day.

Questions to Ask Yourself

Think about your attitudes to negotiating and answer the following questions:

♦ Am I convinced that I have the right to want what I want?

♦ Am I confident of my own case?

♦ Do I keep my ultimate goal in view?

♦ Do I appreciate that there is no deal in the world I cannot do without?

♦ Do I exhibit a positive attitude?

♦ Do I behave reasonably?

♦ Am I prepared to adapt if an equal, but different, deal is offered?

♦ Do I show appreciation when people go some way to meet my needs?

You Will Be Doing Better If...

★ You are convinced of your right to want what you want.

★ You believe in your case.

★ You keep your aims in mind throughout the negotiation.

★ You know there is no deal you cannot do without.

★ You demonstrate a positive attitude.

★ You behave in a reasonable way.

★ You are prepared to adapt when the situation warrants it.

★ You show appreciation when people go some way to meet you.

Check List for Negotiating

If you are finding that negotiating is proving more arduous than you expected, consider whether this is because you could have missed out on one or more aspects of the process, as follows:

Understanding Negotiating

If you find negotiating becoming rather one-sided and you do not seem to be achieving very much, it could be you have not fully appreciated that you have your own source of power. Or possibly you have let yourself fall into a 'win-lose' situation and are not working towards a 'win-win' situation. You need to recognize that you are unlikely to succeed if all you want to do is win.

Preparing

If you are not sure what you will settle for, you may not have prepared thoroughly enough – if at all. Perhaps you did not work out your fall-back position and got trapped into a deal you did not want, or conceivably you made no attempt to identify what others wanted so you were unable to see their point of view. Making sure that you work out exactly what you want means that you will be able to recognize a good deal especially when it turns up unexpectedly.

Negotiating

If you have had a tough time negotiating or you failed to make a deal, it could be because you did not listen to the other people's proposals properly so they did not listen to yours. It is possible that you failed to ask questions or to verify the answers you got. Perhaps you lost a golden opportunity because you did not spot when others shifted their ground. Or maybe you were not prepared to compromise when this would have been beneficial all round.

Troubleshooting

If the negotiation came to a dead end or got out of hand, it could have been that both sides lost sight of the main objectives. Or perhaps you failed to act as a calming influence on unruly behaviour, or even neglected to control your own.

Your Attitude to Negotiating

If you did not achieve what you hoped for, it may be that you were not totally convinced of your case, or you did not feel you had the right to ask for what you want. Possibly you were not in the right frame of mind and therefore lost sight of your purpose. Making sure you keep your aims in view means you stand a better chance of getting a good result every time.

The Benefits of Negotiating

Negotiating provides a framework in which issues can be discussed and explored, compromise achieved, and needs fulfilled. It is the process of trying to get what you want while enabling other people to get what they want.

The benefits you get from negotiating are that:

- You get a chance to voice your requirements in a situation designed for the purpose.

- You give others a better idea of your requirements and get a better idea of theirs.

- You learn a great deal about handling people.

- You obtain co-operation and commitment.

- You establish good working relationships where none have existed, and improve existing ones.

- You reach agreement and satisfy various needs.

- You find out that what you think you need, is often not necessarily what you really need.

Best of all, after you have succeeded in reaching an agreement, the specific benefit of the deal for which you have been negotiating will take effect.

Glossary

Here are some definitions relating to negotiating.

Agreement – Reaching consensus, provided that what everyone consents to is the same.

Compromise – Being willing to keep negotiations going by making mutual concessions.

Conviction – Necessary belief in your own case.

Curbing – Restraining others' feelings by restraining your own.

Deadlock – A standstill resulting from the opposition of equally uncompromising attitudes.

A Deal – A satisfactory settlement for all concerned.

Fall-back – What you will do if you are not offered your basic requirements; also termed BATNA (Best Alternative to a Negotiated Agreement).

Negotiating – Establishing how much you are prepared to give and take. Make sure to take as much as you give and vice versa.

Offer (in your interest) – A proposal for discussion; usually the upper reaches of what you will accept, not necessarily what you will settle for.

Offer (in their interest) – The first lure; a proposal which usually leaves much to be desired.

Position – Point of view, or block of fast-setting concrete, depending on your point of view.

Power – The possession of control, authority, influence, expertise and even a cheerful disposition. Much more important than is recognized, but much less intimidating than the term would suggest.

Preparing – Working out the details beforehand.

Proposals – Different courses of action, each one of which is worth considering.

Questioning – Getting more information and clarifying answers.

Side/Party – The other lot; the person or persons who are dealing with you.

Verifying – Double-checking that what you have understood is actually what others meant.

The Author

Kate Keenan is a Chartered Occupational Psychologist with degrees in affiliated subjects (B.Sc., M.Phil.) and a number of qualifications in others.

She founded Keenan Research, an industrial psychology consultancy, in 1978. The work of the consultancy is fundamentally concerned with helping people to achieve their potential and make a better job of their management.

By devising work programmes for companies she enables them to target and remedy their managerial problems – from personnel selection and individual assessment to team building and attitude surveys. She believes in giving priority to training the managers to institute their own programmes, so that their company resources are developed and expanded.

Kate Keenan enters negotiations knowing precisely what she wants, and with a pretty good idea of what others want. However, she finds that because she is in the business of helping other people to get what they want, she has difficulty in preventing herself becoming more involved in seeking the best possible deal for their requirements than for her own.

THE MANAGEMENT GUIDES

Available now:

	Book £2.99	Tape £4.99
Communicating	☐	
Delegating	☐	
Making Time★	☐	☐
Managing★	☐	☐
Managing Yourself★	☐	☐
Motivating★	☐	☐
Negotiating	☐	
Planning★	☐	☐
Running Meetings	☐	
Selecting People★	☐	☐
Solving Problems	☐	
Understanding Behaviour	☐	

These books are available at your local bookshop or newsagent, or can be ordered direct. Prices and availability are subject to change without notice. Just tick the titles you require and send a cheque or postal order for the value of the book to:

B.B.C.S., P.O. Box 941, HULL HU1 3VQ (24 hour Telephone Credit Card Line: 01482 224626), and add for postage & packing:

UK (& BFPO) Orders: £1.00 for the first book & 50p for each extra book up to a maximum of £2.50. Overseas (& Eire) Orders: £2.00 for the first book, £1.00 for the second & 50p for each additional book.

★These books are also available on audio tape by sending a cheque or postal order for the value of the tape to: Sound FX, The Granary, Shillinglee Park, Chiddingfold, Surrey GU8 4TA (Telephone: 01428 654623; Fax: 01428 707262), and add for postage & packing the same amount as specified for each book, as per above.